REVELATIONS II

A Layman's Reasoning For Mysteries In The Holy Bible

An Alternative View

D. J. NORRIS

First published in Great Britain by
Pen Press Publishers Ltd
39-41, North Road
Islington
London N7 9DP

ISBN 1 900796 67 8

A catalogue record of this book is available from the
British Library

Cover Design by
Bridget Tyldsley Design

REVELATIONS II

A Layman's Reasoning For Mysteries In The Holy Bible

An Alternative View

D. J. NORRIS

Dedication

I wish to dedicate this book to my wife
Lilian Margaret Norris.

About The Author

Douglas John Norris was born in Dover, Kent in 1934. He served in the Royal Air Force for twenty-four years before joining the Ministry of Defence Police. In 1989 he retired to the Algarve, where he still lives, spending his time contemplating the mysteries of life, the universe and the Holy Bible. He has developed a profound interest in environmental issues,  particularly the damage man is doing to the Earth and its long-term effects.

Could a superior species (God's) have genetically engineered the early archetype of young female ape, and did it, after years of evolution, result in the mankind we know today?

Contents

Noah and the Ark

I think most of us remember this story from our childhood - *"and the animals came two by two."*

Let us refresh our memories from the Holy Bible Text:

GENESIS 6

When man had increased in numbers... The Lord saw how wickedness on Earth had become and that every inclination of the thought of his heart had become evil all the time.

The Lord was grieved that HE had made

man on Earth and that every inclination of the thought of his heart had become evil all the time.

The Lord was grieved that he had made man on Earth and his heart was filled with pain.

So the Lord said, "I will wipe mankind whom I have created from the face of the Earth. Men and animals and creatures that move along the ground and the birds of the air..."

But Noah found favour in the eyes of the Lord.

Noah was a righteous man, blameless amongst the people of his time...

God saw how corrupt the Earth had become...

So God said to Noah, "I am going to put an end to all people... So make yourself an Ark of cypress wood, make rooms in it and coat it inside and out with pitch...

*"You are to bring two of every kind *of bird, every kind of animal and every kind of*

*The animals CAME two by two.

2

creature that moves along the ground that will come to you.

You are to take with you every type of food that is to be eaten and store it away as food for you and them."

God must have thought again because he then said:

"Take with you seven of every kind of clean animal and two of every kind of unclean animal."
'Clean' meant roughly any animal whose hoof was completely divided, any bird that did not fly and all fish that had fish scales.
'Unclean' food was anything other than these and, of course, the pig.

"Seven days *from now I will send rain on the Earth for forty days and for forty nights and I will wipe from the face of the Earth every living creature that I have made."

I can only conclude that this is an error or that God'S days are not as ours.

* Seven days to build the ark!

Let us now consider the Ark itself.

I was very pleased to see that in the modern Holy Bible it does not mention cubits. These have been converted into feet. We are told that the Ark was to be:

450ft long
75ft wide
45ft high

Let us now compare this with one of the smaller cruise ships - 10,000 tons, 500 passengers, 200 staff and crew.

498ft long
61ft wide

Now consider this cruise ship in the Dockyard before the passenger cabins, lounges, bars, shops and casino had been fitted. Yes it covers quite a huge area. But you will note that the Ark was wider. Now what about height?

The Ark would have had no need of a promenade deck, sun decks or swimming pools. So the internal area of the Ark would have been even bigger! What a colossal enterprise!

A church minister has insisted that the Ark

was built solely by Noah's family. Someone else has told me no one would work for Noah because they thought he was mad!

I think they could both be wrong!

Just imagine the size of the job. No dockyard, no heavy machinery. No, there must have been a bigger workforce.

I do not think Noah was a rich man. He would not have been able to pay wages, so why would men work for him? For one reason only, the primal instinct of mankind: self preservation!

Because of the size of the project, some of the men must have realized that they might die before its completion, so why? Perhaps they had been working alongside two sons and it was their survival that they were thinking about.

Obviously they were thinking about jumping aboard the Ark when the time came.

Why should they be allowed to?

If they believed Noah's reasons for wanting the Ark built - to obey God's word - they acknowledged the existence of God.

God is a very benevolent God. This belief was probably enough to save them.

What, though, of their wives? They must have believed as well. Can you imagine any wife allowing her husband to work on a madman's project for years and years?

So the Ark was completed and Noah had it provisioned, as with any ship.

I think it would have been impossible for Noah, his family and workers to BRING the animals two by two.

You only have to consider recent TV documentaries showing conservationists capturing endangered species in order to move them to safe parks. They use tranquilizer darts, they rope the legs together. They also use cranes, helicopters and large lorries.

So why did the animals *come* two by two?

I have long been convinced that God's species have the power of telepathy; not only between themselves but also with man. If one of the characters in the Holy Bible says: "God spoke to me and said" he could be quite right. Those words were 'put' into his head. They were not any inspiration of his own.

This 'power' of God' species, when it came to animals, with their smaller, less intelligent brains, would, I think, be nothing less that absolute 'mind control'.

This is how I think the animals were brought to the Ark.

I also think that this 'mind control' continued throughout the time that the Ark was afloat; otherwise it would have been absolute bedlam on board!

The animals and creatures would have been subdued, but that's all. The chickens would still have laid eggs, the others would have carried on reproducing. They would, of course, have had to be fed, and the all important mucking out would have needed to be done.

This would have taken a small army: another reason why I think the workers and their families were on board.

I felt that long before the animals came, Noah would have realized that his family alone could not have coped.

I think that during the building of the Ark Noah gave orders for extra human accommodation to be added.

Remember this was God's 'RESTART' for mankind.

If it had been only Noah's family on board there could have been serious problems due to interbreeding, as we are all aware of these days.

The Ark is Finished and the Animals are Aboard

The first drops of rain fell. The Holy Bible tells us it rained for forty days and forty nights.

Rain only, no suggestion of any storms, so the Ark would have been stable.

After forty days the skies cleared and the whole of Earth was covered with water.

The Ark was afloat for one year and they must have had many problems.

Some of the beasts were meat eaters. There would have been no problem with their food, though it could have been left alive until required. Eggs might have been one kind of food for the snakes and other reptiles. Those that chewed the cud would have had to make do with straw. There would have been seeds for the birds.

But what of mankind? They would not have been allowed by their religious law to eat raw meat, as blood could not pass their lips.

God had told Noah to coat the inside of the Ark with pitch.

I am sure, though, that Noah had thought about this and had left an area clear. The Ark would have had the equivalent of any ship's galley (plenty of buckets of water around no doubt).

Also, I think Noah might have used earth a balast.

Once the rains had stopped there was no need for any more. Perhaps the carpenters on board opened up part of the roof and, using some of the earth from the ballast, constructed a 'roof garden'. If they had seeds, they could have grown some green vegetables there

All in all, it must have been an ordeal. But how happy they must have been that they survived!

And how happy *we* must be!

GENESIS 8

"After the flood Noah built an altar to the Lord and, taking some of the clean animals and clean birds, he sacrificed them as a burnt offering on it."

The Burning Bush

EXODUS 2.8

Now Moses was tending the flock of Jethro, his father-in-law, and he led the flock to the far side of the desert, and came to the mountain of God. Then the Angel of God appeared to him in the flames within a bush.

Moses saw that although the bush was on fire it did not burn up.

When the Lord saw that Moses had gone over to look, He called to him from within the bush:

"Moses, Moses."

And Moses said, "Here I am."

"Do not come any closer," God said. *"I have come down to rescue my people from the hand of Egypt."*

What was the purpose of the burning bush? This effect, in my opinion, could have easily been created by God's species with their advanced technical knowledge.

But why a burning bush?
Why does a town crier have a bell!
It was to draw MOSES' attention!
"Moses hid his face because he was afraid to look at God."

In this case I feel he would have had no reason to be afraid.

God appeared as a Hologram (a three dimensional figure that can move and talk), hence his often repeated instruction:

"Do not come any closer." Why this instruction?

Because a Hologram has no physical structure. Moses would, I suggest, have seen an elderly man with a benevolent expression on his face, and long white hair and a white beard.

The Tablets of the Ten Commandments

Moses was told by God to climb to the top of Mount Sinai (Telepathy).

There he received the two tablets of the Commandments that God had brought down with.

EXODUS 34.22

"Then Moses said, 'Now show me your Glory.' And the Lord said, 'I will cause all my goodness to pass in front of you, and I will proclaim my name, The Lord, in your

presence. I will have mercy on whom I have mercy and I will have compassion on whom I have compassion.

But' he said, 'You cannot see my face, for no one may see my face and live.'

"The Lord continued, 'There is a place near me where you may stand on a rock. When my glory passes by I will put you in a cleft in the rock, and cover you with my hand until I have passed by. Then I will remove my hand and you will see my back, but my face must not be seen!'"

Why should MOSES not look upon God's face if he had appeared to him before?

Why now was it *"if any man see my face he will not live"?*

What was different?

I suggest that this time the stone tablets were the difference.

The appearance of God in human form on previous occasions was as a Hologram. These have no physical form and cannot carry physical objects.

This time God had to come as 'himself', a different species from mankind. Mankind was born of apes by Divine Intervention (see *REVELATIONS I*) and because of this he has a close resemblance to the apes. It is now less and less because of the known evolution of man.

I think God's species look entirely different from us!

I do not believe that if MOSES or any other man had seen God's face at this time he would have died.

Certainly there would have been, as I have previously suggested, fear and panic.

It seems, however, that God was determined that Moses should not see his face by literally putting the fear of 'God' in him!

Author's note.

During my researches, I had reason to speak to a muslim. In an encyclopedia I found that their Koran forbade them from drawing a picture or making any model or statue of Allah, depicting him as a man or animal.

Forget animal; I think that went out with the Egyptians. But what about man?

The answer I received was, *"No man knows what Allah (God) looks like!"*

When I said, *"I agree with you,"* I wish you could have seen the muslim's face. He certainly didn't expect that from a Christian!

The Empty Tomb

The Israelites had been under the yoke of Roman occupation for many years. They had to pay taxes to the Roman Authorities.

At the time of Jesus's birth there was a census which required them to return to the towns of their birth.

The Israelites had long prayed to 'God' to release them from their ordeal.

They were convinced 'God' would do this as he had released their ancestors from the bondage of Egypt. They believed that 'God' would send them a warrior king who would lead them to overthrow the Roman occupation of their land.

The Roman Authorities must have been aware of this. They would have been backed by the Roman Army, which, like any army, would have had their Intelligence Corps. I think they would have opened a file on this threat before Jesus's birth.

When Jesus was born they must have been aware of the visit by the three kings even to the extent of knowing the gifts they bore.

They must have watched Jesus throughout his childhood, increasing their surveilance as he grew to adulthood.

Once he started to gather support (his disciples) the Romans may well have donned the garb of his supporters and joined the crowd.

How surprised they must have been when they heard the suspected leader of the Jews telling his people:

"If a man strike you on your left cheek offer him your right cheek."

"If you see a stranger, even if not of your race or religion, in need of help, assist him."

"Love your enemy."

How surprised they must have been , and how confused the superiors must have been.

They must have also been surprised and interested when Jesus went to the Temple.

MATTHEW 20.18

"Jesus entered the Temple area and drove out all who were buying and selling there. He overturned the table of the money changers and the benches of those selling doves. He said,

'It is written, My House will be called a House of Prayer but you are making it a House of Robbers.' "

The Roman surveilance team may well have been alarmed at his anger. But when they reported this occurrence to their superiors, there appears to have been no public support, and so they decided it was not their problem.

Certainly for the High Priests of the Temple it was a problem.

I think it was more than probable that they were receiving rent from the table owners and a commission from the money-changers.

They were also consumed with envy. Here

was this man dressed in simple clothes with dusty feet attracting a multitude of their people to listen to his teaching.

They themselves were probably dressed in scarlet with gold piping and ornate head gear.

This was enough reason for them to hate Jesus and want to kill him. They determined to persuade the Elders of the tribe to support them.

LUKE 21.36

Now the feast of the unleavened bread called The Passover was approaching and the Chief Priests and the teachers of the Law (Elders) were looking for some way to get rid of Jesus, for they were afraid of Him.

Yes! Jesus was becoming far too popular for their liking.

As for the Roman Authorities, although they were surprised at Jesus's anger at the Temple, their major concern was that the population would rise up against them.

Jesus was betrayed and arrested by the priests of Roman soldiers and bought before Pilate.

MARK 15.7

Now it was the custom at the Feast to release any prisoner the people requested.

A man called Barabas was in prison for murder. The crowd came up and asked Pilate to do for them what he usually did.

"Do you want me to release to you the King of the Jews?" said Pilate, knowing it was out of envy that the High Priests had handed Jesus to him.

But the High Priests stirred up the crowd to have Pilate release Barabas instead.

"What shall I do then with the one you call King of the Jews?" Pilate asked them.

"Crucify him!" they shouted.

"What crime has he committed?" asked Pilate.

But they shouted all the louder *"Crucify him."*

Wanting to satisfy the crowd Pilate released Barabas to them. He had Jesus flogged and handed him over to be crucified.

Jesus was duly crucified. His body was then placed in a tomb on a hillside, its entrance covered with a large stone.

MATTHEW 28.16

The next day the priests went to see Pilate. *"Sir,"* they said, *"we remember that while he was still alive the decivar said, 'After three days I will arise again.'"*

"So give orders for the tomb to be made secure until the third day, otherwise his Disciples may steal the body and tell the people he has been raised from the dead."

This was done and on the third day the tomb was found empty.

Some of the guards went into the city and reported to the Chief Priests.

When the Chief Priest met with the Elders they devised a plan. They gave the soldiers a large sum of money telling them they were to go to Pilate and say, *"His Disciples came during the night when we were asleep."* If this report went to Pilote it would satisfy him.

This plan has me puzzled, because this is what they were afraid of in the first place, maybe they were concerned that no blame should fall on their shoulders.

I think, however, that the High Priests were far nearer the truth than they thought.

If the soldier guards were paid by the High Priests, and this seems likely, they would have wanted payment in advance.

A soldier on night duty, bored, with little chance of supervision, and money in his pocket, would certainly obtain a bottle of something to help him through the long hours. Not only would they have slept but they would have also been slightly drunk.

Jesus's disciples knew that the High Priests hated and envied Jesus and that the last thing they would have wanted was for him to become a martyr and for his tomb to become a shrine.

The Roman Authorities would have known this, but their major concern would have been the crowd's anger.

I feel that the disciples were afraid that because of this the tomb might be desecrated and detroyed.

Then, as the High Priests had feared, when the guards were asleep they opened the tomb, removed Jesus's body and re buried it in a secluded secret location - never found.

When Jesus died on the cross his soul left him.

While all this was going on Jesus was in 'Heaven', trying to persuade 'His' 'Father', 'God', not to Destroy the Earth and all mankind by taking all the blame for his own death and mankind's sins upon himself.

We should all be thankful that he succeeded.

For he is surely our Saviour.

The Search for the Holy Grail

O ver the centuries there have been many searches to find the Holy Grail.

MATTHEW 26.26

"Then he took the cup, gave thanks and offered it to them saying, 'Drink from it, all of you. This is my blood of the covenant and is poured out for the forgiveness of sins. I tell you that I will not drink of this fruit of the vine until that day when I drink it anew, with you, in my Father's Kingdom.'"

(All right, All right! I can almost hear the cries of 'cheers'.) Alcohol in Heaven! Why not? Some people may be aghast at this. Some of these may be the ones who suggest every word in the Holy Bible is God's word!

Because of this people have been searching, hoping to find this chalice or cup.

There have been arguments as to whether it was made of wood or gold.

Later people re-considered Jesus's words and the word GRAIL. Could this have been a 'container' of his blood?

Again the searches continued.

Much later it was suggested that this container of Jesus's blood was taken from Jerusalem by Mary of Magdelene and that she fled to GAUL (FRANCE).

It has also been suggested that she herself was the container - that she was pregnant by Jesus!!

It was also thought that this SECRET of SECRETS was covered up by no less than the Crusaders of RICHARD COEUR DE LION (RICHARD THE LIONHEART), French nobles and French priests.

This secret was so important that any revelation of it would mean death to the informant.

It is also suggested that in France there is a French nobleman's chateau with outbuilding that could have been the Crusaders' barracks.

Recently it has been claimed that an ancient grave flagstone has been found with the name and dates obliterated.

Could this have been the grave of Mary of Magdelene or one of her successors?

As far as I know, no explanation of these suggestions has been given.

Before we consider, what this would mean to Christianity if it were true, let us once again consult the Holy Bible.

Jesus was travelling with his Disciples to Jerusalem for the Feast of the Passover. They were tired and in need of refeshment.

LUKE 10.36

"As Jesus and his disciples were on their way. He came to a village where a woman

called Martha opened her door to him.

She had a sister called Mary who sat at the Lord's feet listening to what he said.

But Martha was distracted by all the preparations that had to be made. She came to him and asked, 'Lord do you not care that my sister has left me to do the work by myself. Tell her to help me.'

'Martha, Martha,' the Lord answered. 'You are worried about many things. But the only thing needed, Mary, has chosen, what is better it will not be taken from her.'"

Was this village called Magdelene? Mary has been referred to in the HOLY BIBLE as Mary of Magdclcne.

Was this the first meeting of Jesus and Mary?

Let us now consider of Bible text.

MATTHEW 28.16

"Many women were watching at a distance (The crucifixion).

They had followed Jesus from Galilee. Amongst them were Mary of Magdelene,

Martha, the mother of James, Joseph and the mother of Zebedee's sons."
MARK 16.20

When the Sabbath was over, Mary of Magdelene, Mary the mother of James and Solame went with spices so that they might go and anoint Jesus's body.

The tomb was Empty.

LUKE 24.19

When they came back from the tomb they told all these things to the eleven and all the others.

It was Mary of Magdelene and the others who told the apostles.

JOHN 20.23

Then the disciples went back to their homes. But Mary of Magdelene stood outside the tomb crying.

"Woman," a man said, *"why are you crying? Who is it that you are looking for?"*

Thinking he was a gardener, she said, *"Sir, if you have taken him away tell me where you have put him and I will get him?"*

Jesus (for it was Him) said to her, *"Mary."* She turned to him and he cried out, *"Do not (attempt to) hold on to me."*

Mary of Magdelene ran to tell the disciples with the news. *"I have seen the Lord!*

Now, let us consider the actions of Mary of Magdelene. Does she seem like an ordinary supporter? No! Perhaps a woman in love?

Consider also Jesus's words: *"Mary, do not hold me."*

Jesus appeared to her as a Hologram. (His own body was already decaying).

However this word 'HOLD' entrigues me.

During all His other appearances he gave the instruction: *'Do not approach me'*.

Does this 'HOLD' suggest a closer relationship?

Jesus was born of woman, as we all are. He was different from us because his father was God, but nonetheless he was born as a man.

He must have known joy and sorrow. When he ejected the money exchangers from the temple, he expressed anger. He must also have experienced despair.

Could it be possible, therefore, that before the end of his life he found the love of a woman and returned it?

Before we consider the effects this would have, if any, on Christianity if it were true, let us return to consider Mary of Magdelene.

The High Priests of the temple must have felt pleased that they had got rid of Jesus.

However, they must have kept a close watch on the disciples and all associated with them.

One would have been Mary of Magdelene. If she was pregnant, as with any woman, this would have soon become noticeable.

The temple priest would probably have arrested her and asked her who was the father. Mary would have refused to answer until the priest reminded her of the law: if she refused to answer their questions they would accuse her of adultery. The penalty for this was stoning! Not a pleasant way to die.

Mary must have been terrified and admitted that Jesus was the father!

How this must have alarmed the High Priests! They had just got rid of Jesus and now they had what could become an even bigger problem on their hands.

They had to get rid of this girl, and fast.

How could they cause her to vanish without any comeback?

We have already learnt that money seemed no problem. They had already bribed the guards of Jesus's tomb with a large sum.

In this case, I think they also contacted the Roman Authorities and suggested Mary of Magdelene was their problem too.

It would seem to have been quite easy to exile Mary. Even in those days there would have been trade, and a large bribe to a ship's captain would have achieved the result they wanted.

It seems that this is what happened.

So, what about the effects on Christianity if any of this is proved true?

I don't think any of us have to worry. I hope you will agree with me that if this is so,

then Jesus becomes more human, and we can
identify with him more easily

For me, instead of reducing my respect for
him, it would increase it.

Healing

Over the years many people have claimed to be healers.

Many claim that by laying on their hands they can relieve pain and other symptons.

How can this be?

Some claim they are gathering cosmic forces, others that they are a conduit for God.

In this case, I think they are partially right.

Mankind was born of ape by divine intervention. Mankind is genetically part man and part God's species. God's species are far more intelligent and scientifically advanced than mankind.

They have the capability of healing species other than their own.

This capability is very weak in mankind and not evident to most of us. However, it seems that some people are aware of this power and seem to be able to use it.

Why have I come to this conclusion?

Let us consider the actions of Jesus.

Jesus was born of woman, the Holy Mother Mary, once again by divine intervention. Unlike mankind Jesus was not born of ape. He was born of evolved mankind.

This means that, although in appearance he was a man, he was unlike any man before him.

The God species was very powerful in Him and he was, as any Bible tells us, able to heal the blind, lame, and those with other afflictions by the 'laying on' of his hands.

It is reported that he raised LAZARUS from the dead. The Bible tells us that it wasn't until four days after LAZARUS' death that Jesus reached his tomb, and that LAZARUS appeared at the entrance alive again when Jesus called him.

34

I reserve judgement on this. I think LAZARUS could have been in a coma and the distraught family did not know the difference.

Certainly, then, Jesus's telepathic and 'mind control' powers could have brought LAZARUS back to consciousness. However, this is only a theory.

Jesus certainly possessed powers beyond our comprehension. (My own doctor has confirmed that after four days, the brain would have been dead and vital organs would have started to decay. He said, *"In some cases only a known voice is enough to bring someone out of a coma."*)

Spiritualists

Over the years spiritualists have received a bad name in the press and TV because of some charlatan mediums who are adept at finding out pet names and other idiosyncrasies of their clients' departed relatives.

If they do this to convince their clients that they are in contact with a 'loved one', this is fraud. If they charge for this service they are despicable.

Not all spiritualists sit in a dim light holding hands or with a finger on a glass.

Over the years I have had two friends who said they were Christian spiritualists.

They claimed their sole interest was in spiritual healing and saving lost souls.

Lost souls?

How can this be? They both told me that at death the soul leaves the body. If the death is sudden or violent the soul does not suffer a physical shock but can be confused.

They both told me the same thing. If I were to drop dead at their feet, I would stand there looking at my body and ask them, "What has happened?" They said they wouldn't see or hear me and I wouldn't understand why they didn't answer me.

They said if I was lucky, someone I had previously known who had died would appear at my shoulder and lead me away.

I don't know about that, but it seems probable that after a violent, unexpected death, the soul could be confused and not make its way to Heaven.

It could, in fact, wander around and become lost.

If these spiritualists spend time and trouble trying to help these lost souls, if help is needed, perhaps we should not be so quick to condemn them.

Churches and Cathedrals

When I was about 11 years of age my parents and I returned to the town of Dover in Kent.

We had been evacuated for the duration of the Second World War.

My parents were allocated a prefab on a prefab estate.

I still remember how it looked, although the prefabs have long since gone.

Now that I think about it, the pub was a converted brick house.

The church a wooden hut with a simple wooden cross over the entrance door.

Now I believe any church is the congregation inside, not the building.

In the town of Dover, some of the larger, ornate, brick-built churches survived the shelling.

On a Sunday, was there any difference between these congregations? Of course not; God is not interested in the building.

During the last Great War, your fathers or grandfathers would have held Church Services in North Africa standing in the open on hot sand.

Do you think God was at all bothered about this?

Of course not.

Throughout the world, large churches and cathedrals have been built 'To the Glory of God'.

Are they really neccessary?

In some countries there is a large white church in the centre of each village. This would have been built with money from the ancestors of the poor peasants who are still living in hovels and still paying money for the church's upkeep.

Do you think that God wants this?

After all, all God wants is for each of us to believe in His existence, that He created the

Earth and that he sent his Son to instruct us in the way we should lead our lives.

We do not even need a wooden hut church to do this.

It can be done anywhere, anytime.

You do not even have to speak out aloud. A thought confirming your belief is all that is needed.

I'm not saying God will hear you then. But your soul knows and as long as you maintain this belief, your soul will report this when it is your time to be judged.

If you want to confirm your belief amongst others in 'a house of God' fine, but do not marvel and admire the architecture, statues, gold-leaf and ornate woodwork. If you are in a small village church, with a muddy path and a cold draughty interior, do not complain.

I do not think God is interested in any of these things. But he is interested in you!

Appearances of the Holy Mother Mary

Most of us have heard of the appearance of the Holy Mother to a young peasant girl, Marie Bernarde Soubirous, better known to us as St Bernadette.

This occurred in 1858 in Lourdes.

Fewer may know of the appearance of the Holy Mother to three small children, a boy and two girls Francisco, Jacinta and Lucia, in a small hamlet in West Central Portugal. This is now know as a national shrine for Our Lady of the Rosary of Fatima.

This appearance occurred in 1917. Lucia is still alive, having spent her life in a convent school in Coimbra in the North of Portugal.

She is now too old for convent duty and lives in a retirement home.

However, my interest in these appearances is this:

How did Bernadette recognise the figure as the Holy Mother and when the Holy Mother spoke, how come she understood her?

Similary, how did the Portuguese children recognise the figure of the Holy Mother? How come they understood her?

It seems to me that their recognition can only have come from having seen the statues in their churches. But there is no standard model for statues of the Holy Mother throughout the world.

The statues in France would have looked different from those in Portugal! In France the Holy Mother must have spoken French. In Portugal, she must have spoken Portuguese!

Does this not suggest that God takes an intense interest in us?

Now for a previously unreported, undocumented appearance of the Holy Mother.

A lady came to see me and told me she

felt that she had been saved by the appearance of the Holy Mother. This occurred around 1983/4.

She was sailing solo a 27ft sloop between Guernsey and Alderney in the Channel Isles.

When she set out the sea was calm. However, these waters can change unexpectedly. They did, and as she approached Alderney the seas became choppy. She was also concerned because she heard the sounds of explosions, suggesting demolition work in the area of the harbour ahead of her. She was fighting the sea and could not leave the tiller to go to the cockpit to radio the harbour master about her concern.

She told me that being a Roman Catholic, she said her Hail Marys and suddenly the figure of the Holy Mother appeared, sitting on a seat opposite her in the stern. The Holy Mother did not speak; she simply smiled and faded away a few moments later.

This was enough to give this woman the courage to continue and reach a safe haven soon after.

She tells me that she now regards the Holy Mother as her guardian. Although she has not seen the Holy Mother again during two recent hospital operations, she says she has felt her presence.

A New Planet, Sister Earth?

Scientists have found a previously unknown planet behind the sun. They have reported that it is the same distance from the sun as our own Earth; that is all that they have to say for the moment.

However, let us think about this: the same distance from the sun as our Earth? All planets revolve, so it must have what we call day and night. Not only will it have day and night but they will be of the same duration as ours. The sun will warm the planet during the day and if you or I could stand on it, we would see the same moon and stars we see on Earth!

I think our scientists should forget about trying to put men on Mars or Venus, and investigate this planet further.

What if it has ice-caps, water and is green?
In fact, a sister of Earth?
Why should this be?
God created intelligent beings, us, on our Earth, but he has never been happy with us.

Some people still blame this on the serpent who persuaded Eve to eat the forbidden fruit in the Garden of Eden; and that she persuaded Adam to also eat it and that was where it all went wrong!

I think this is just symbolic. Something certainly went wrong.

God's spirit/soul within us was not 'in control'. From the beginning, mankind has had free will.

Free will was not the problem. I am sure that God's spirit or soul within us or at least our conscience, warns us if we are about to do wrong.

No, it was the gift - if it is a gift - of 'first thought' that has been our downfall.

First thought gave us fire, the spear, the

wheel: benefits, it is true, but what about gunpowder, the bullet, the machine gun, the atom bomb, smart bomb and Cruise missiles?

Do any of you think for one moment this was God's intention? Of course not!

This has been a big mistake. At the moment, our ozone layer is being depleted. This means more cases of skin cancer. Global warming? This sounds good - we could all do with more sunshine. But I'm afraid this is a false surmise. Will we be pleased when this increase causes both the very young and old to die? I think not!

You will all have seen the posters 'Save the Whales', 'Save the Rain forest'. The Friends of the Earth have recently expressed concern at genetically modified food.

These people who say that if we can kill the weeds, kill the insects, kill any blight, you will have unblemished fruit and vegetables.

Do you think for one minute this is why they are doing this?

Think again! For them it means no spoilt fruit or vegetables, no waste, therefore bigger profits! and I'm afraid, *"To Hell with the consequences!"* Friends of the Earth were quite right. Surely all of you are concerned with what sort of world your great and great great grandchildren will inherit?

What can you do? You may say, *"Divided we fall, united we stand."*

I'm afraid your car is one of the major causes of the change in the environment. Is it your fault? Of course not, you have no choice other than to fill the tank with petrol.

France has produced a few - too few in my opinion - electric cars. These are 'green'.

Many of us know that water is H_2O, it's been a question on many quiz shows. What is H_2O? Many of you will remember from your school days that if you pass an electric current through water you produce Hydrogen and Oxygen.

These gasses are explosive, they will certainly propel a car and they are green.

Why do we not have more electric cars and hydrogen cars? Simply because of the vested interest in oil, the vast profits to be made from oil; it is simply greed! Take the money now and to Hell with the future!

No wonder that God has been unhappy with us. But He is a 'Loving God'. How many times has he given us a second chance?

He once decided to kill us all and then relented with the 'fortunate' few on the Ark. Finally he sent what we Christians call 'his son' to tell us how to behave. What happened? 'He' was crucified!

Second chances, to be sure.

Now let us return to this recently discovered Planet.

As I have said, God must despair of us. Something has obviously gone wrong!

Is it possible that God has given himself a second chance?

Has he 'seeded' another planet in our galaxy?

Has He made a fresh start?

Has he realized His mistake. (I'm sorry if I am condemned for saying this; let it be).

Perhaps with 'Plan 2', this time his intelligent beings will be controlled by God's species in them the spirit within them.

What does this mean? Our Ten Commandments, for a start, can be forgotten. On the new planet, they will be obeyed for a start. Doesn't this sound like God's Kingdom on Earth (2)?

Will He abandon us?

I think not, He is a loving God. But are we out of control? It seems that our survival is down to us!!

Questions and Answers

Since I started writing, many of my friends have shown an interest in both my work and my words. They have obviously told others because several people have approached me with questions.

One woman came to see me. Her question was:

"My first husband died soon after our marriage. I married again and have two children and five grandchildren. When I die and my present husband dies, and we go to Heaven, where we might meet my first husband, whose wife will I be?"

I hope she forgave me because I had to smile.

This same question was asked to Jesus on at least three occasions, once by the Elders of the tribe.

Let us consider his reply:

"You have not read the Scriptures. There are no marriages in Heaven neither will any woman be offered in marriage. You are as angels."

The Bible tells us that the people marvelled at his answer. Marvelled? Is it clear to you? I doubt it. So let us consider what he meant.

"You have not read the Scriptures."

There have been many editions of the Holy Bible. The latest, I am pleased to say, dispensed with the words 'Thee', 'Thou' and now incorporates information from the Dead Sea Scrolls. However, if the answer to that woman's question is in any edition of the Holy Bible it is very obscure. So let us leave this and consider.

"There are no marriages in Heaven. Neither will any woman be offered in marriage."

Let us then consider marriage. What was its purpose in the time of Jesus? It was the religious law at that time that if a husband died and no children had been born, it was the duty of one of his unmarried brothers to marry the widow in order to produce children!

So what is Jesus telling us? *"There is no marriage in Heaven"*.

No children will be born in Heaven!

The real answer came with his words.

'You are as angels'.

God's species are entirely different in appearance from us (see *'The delivery of the Tablets of the 10 Commandments'*, when God said, *"No man may see my face and live"*).

When we die our spirit/soul leaves our body. It is the 'God's species' part of our body. But it does not have the human animal sexual organs we humans have.

So was Jesus saying, *"There is no sex in Heaven?"*

(Alright, alright, I was nearly deafened when I suggested there was alcohol in Heaven. Now I can hear a definite murmur of, *"Thank God, I will not have to invent a headache!"*)

Seriously though, jealousy on Earth is due to sex, property or money. As these things do not exist in Heaven. So when this wife meets her two husbands they can all be the best of friends and to use the words of Our Lord, *'love one another'*.

Another man came to see me, a young German. Since birth he had had a speech impediment and a misformed hip joint. Apparently neither can be corrected by medical science at this time.

He was worried that if he died, his spirit/ soul would have the same problems.

I was very pleased to be able to tell him that I believed these afflictions were those of his human animal body only, and that when he died his spirit/soul would be perfect, with no such problems. I also suggested that the blind would see!

Another friend came to me to say that he had found in his edition of the Bible the words:

"The Gods came down and found the women beautiful and married them."

He told me he had had found this in GENESIS. His concern was Gods 'God' in the plural. He apparently had asked two church ministers about this text.

He was told that they didn't know of it. That was their answer! I'm afraid I have found this about the church. If a minister cannot say, *"You must have faith my son"*, they usually change the subject!

I too have been unable to find this text but nonetheless it interests me so let us consider it.

"The Gods came down and found the women beautiful."

I doubt that very much, as I have said God's species are different in appearance from us.

So what is happening here?

My original thought was for 'Gods' read 'Angels' and for 'women' read 'young female ape' - the birth of mankind! But I realized this was too easy and there was more to it than that.

Let us consider the man who wrote these words.

Mankind had come a long way. This man was intelligent; he had language, speech and could read. He would not know, however, about the evolution of mankind (I don't think they started digging up the bones until far later).

He would have thought that the men and women had always been as he saw them. I think I might have found a soulmate. He was obviously unhappy about the Scriptures. Look at the story of how God created ADAM and, while he slept, took a rib from his chest and created EVE.

They had two sons. Cain and Abel. We are told that Cain killed Abel. God was angry and told Cain to go forth, his crops would fail and the thorns would tear his flesh. The next thing that happens is that Cain's wife appears on the scene! Where did she come from? (Try asking a Church minister about that!)

No this man was unhappy, he realized that there would have had to be several 'ADAMs and 'EVEs. Did not the Scriptures list unlawful sex? Surely sex between close family was unlawful?

According to those laws the human race would never have got off the ground with just one man and one woman. H solved the first part of the problem by putting the woman (females) in the plural. BUT he then had a problem. The Scriptures told him that God created mankind.

Unfortunately for him there was only God at that time, he would not have thought of God as a member of another species.

So what could the poor fellow do? Probably by this time he was at his wits' end and could do nothing but put an 's' after God to satisfy his problem.

My friend, by the way, still wants an answer from a church minister. I think he will have to wait a long time!

Another woman came to see me and asked why children die young? I asked her if this had happened to her. She replied that her daughter, aged five, had been knocked down by a drunken driver and died before reaching the hospital. I asked her if she had asked a church minister about this, and she said she had.

What did he say? Surprise, Surprise: *"It was God's Will"*.

I asked her if she believed this, and she said, *"No"*.

I agreed with her and said, *"Mankind are like the grains of sand on a seashore. God cannot watch over all of us every second, minute or hour of every day. Your daughter's death was the result of human error. Have any of your daughter's grandparents died?"*

"Yes, my father died when she was two years old."

I then said, *"Do not despair, she is now with your father. I think he may well have spoiled her here on Earth, but whether he can spoil her in Heaven I am not sure. However, for Heaven read 'love'. She will certainly be loved and have many companions of her own age."*

I'm afraid to say that the woman cried and so did I! Why did I say this. Let's consider Jesus's words:

"Suffer little children to come unto me."

Many of us are familiar with this but what about what follows?

"You cannot enter the Kingdom of Heaven unless you are as a child."

What did Jesus mean?

I think that a young child is innocent of sin. We do not sin until we reach adulthood.

If we cannot enter Heaven other than as a child, we have problems!

All that is necessary is for you to repent your sins.

If you are a rich man, God requires you to forget about successors and donate your wealth to charity if you wish to enter the Kingdom of Heaven.

Research Documents

Reader's Digest Great Illustrated
Dictionary
All Holy Bible Text taken from The New
International version, 1980 Edition
The Koran
Private interviews as stated